DORSET DAYS

An Anthology of Poetry

By

Ray Wills

A Gypsy poet production

List of poems featured here are written by Ray Wills

Wareham Town Days -WAREHAM

On Canford Magna road -POOLE

Those were the days of Gypsy lore

Travellers Lament

Living in New England -KINSON

Coy Meadows - BOURNEMOUTH

Swanage - SWANAGE

Gypsy days and nights

In Newtown Childhood Days - POOLE

Rossmore Days - POOLE

Brick makers of old Newtown - POOLE

Carey camp -WAREHAM

Purbeck – THE PURBECK

Th Square and the Compass – WORTH MATRAVERS
SWANAGE

Winfrith Village life -WINFRITH

Judge Jeffries - DORCHESTER

Sugar Knobb- POOLE

Such Majesty

Queen of the Castles and Kings - POOLE

Augustus John and the Gypsies -ALDERNEY

Talbots two sisters -TALBOT VILLAGE

Brownsea Island boys -BROWNSEA

The last knocker upper of Poole - POOLE

Roma Day in Dorchester - DORCHESTER

Gypsy flower girls dreams - BOURNEMOUTH

Vardo Days

Treasury of Dorset

Old Poole Town - POOLE

Dorset

Home at last

Gullivers Days -KINSON

My Dorset

Wareham Lad - WAREHAM

The back streets of Poole -POOLE

Dorset past times

Dorset Steam Fair - BLANDFORD

Sea View Parkstone -POOLE

The Snakes gone - NEWTOWN POOLE

Wareham - WAREHAM

Westbourne Tales -BOURNEMOUTH

Dorset Gypsies

The kids who Conker-ed Dorset - HOLTON
HEATH/WAREHAM

Dorset Breed

Bluebird Caravans - NEWTOWN POOLE

One of the Lads

The Batman - BOVINGTON WAREHAM

School Days - NEWTOWN POOLE

Gypsy Lad -NEWTOWN POOLE

Acknowledgements

Art pictures are courtesy of the artist Dawn Jeanette Grant Harrison.

The Photos are courtesy of Owen Tuckett and Sharon Muiruri Coyne (originally used in the film GHOST GYPSY). Betty Blue Smith Packman Billington of Kushti Bok, Steve Royce Rogers, Sally Slocombe, Kevin Crocker,Terry Andrews, Lynda Stuchberry and Dorchester Museum.

All poetry is the sole work of Ray Wills who is best known as the Gypsy Poet.

Previous publications by Raymond Wills include The Gypsy Storyteller Anthology of poetry, Where the River Bends, Romance in the Everglades Anthology of poetry, Ventures in Childs Play, The Gypsy Camp.

Mannings Heath

We lived here in the vast fertile common lands known as Canford Heath which at one time in the 15th century had encompassed some 38,000 acres of land owned by the aristocracy. Our encampment was in an area of fern heath land, known as New England. An area which had Turbary rights, dating ways back to the Doomsday book of 1000. Rights which included the grazing of cattle and the cutting and gathering of peat for fires such as at the Turbary common lands. Our encampment was situated within a village parish known then as Kinson. We lived here with our extended families of parents and offspring of chavvies, Grand parents, Elders, cousins and friends amongst the silver birch, yellow furze and heather. A horde of Gypsy Travellers encampments evolved from around the early 1800s throughout these Canford Parish common lands. With close to forty or more by the early 20th century. These all were very different in size and numbers with extremely unusual names. Names which included the following list-Cuckoo bottom, Frying pan,heavenly bottom etc.

Our small strip of land now known as "New England" was just one of many similar encampments on the heathlands of Kinson village in greater Canford. It was given its name by our own Gypsy travelling folki from the New Forest who favoured it amongst all of the scores of Canford encampments. Many of our forefathers had their origins in the new forest and other areas of the land which was then mainly forests. For it reminded them of the Forests itself. Some of our fore bearers such as the Stanley's had left for a new life as horse breeders and farmers in the new worlds of America and Australia of their own choosing. Though history shows that so many of our folki were exploited as slaves or sent to prisons in the new world often deported for very petty crimes such as catching rabbits or trespassing on the Lords estate. They having little monies were often unable to pay fines to the magistrates courts often he himself was the landowner. As a result they were sent to work on plantations or on convict ships to Australia imprisoned for numerous crimes from simple poaching of rabbits, horse theft to assault. Our community of Travellers despite our in built wanderlust had been loyal to our country with many being active in the armed services through numerous wars and campaigns. We were particularly loyal to the farmers who depended upon our labour each season of crops and fruit picking. Then Britannia one of the young women present spoke up " Hey Sam any news on the Hughes family at Corfe Mullen, do they still live on the "Downy" encampment on Colonel Georges land by the woods there and is Caroline still there and does she still sing all those old songs". I quickly responded "Yes Britannia, Aaron and I visited them just recently they are still there and we saw Colonel George and had a pleasant chat with him". "He told us he is keen to employ workers in brick to build a new town on the large heathlands by the Bourne river estuary which we know as Poole heath. He said that he plans to start work there sometime in the future". "He will need good brick makers, craftsman and labourers for the brickyards he owns". I looked into the burning red glint of the fire and told them "You know years ago the gentry at Corfe Mullen had plantations and labouring slaves working there. Many of these were young Gypsy lads and in later years lots of these fellows were shipped to Newfoundland as apprentices to the slave masters and the cod industries. This sort of thing went on in many areas in Dorset over the years such as at Bere Regis under the rich Drax estate as well as the nearby Framptons, Lees, Welds and others".

The babes and chavvies were tucked up in their beds tonight, it had been a long day and tonight the folki were enjoying the comradeship of the occasion. Along with the evening, the fire and the starlit night sky. Talk was also of the morrow the illnesses of the clan and the deals done in town with the bartering of pony sales and at the market place. The evening continued likewise but interrupted only occasionally by the occasional sounds of a concertina small piano accordion played by the nimble fingers of one of its members a Clapcott Gypsy lad and the dancing of the Smith Gal's.

We worked on their farms each year for which they allowed us to park in their farmlands, to camp our tents, wagons and benders. Soe of us bought the land or came to mutual arrangement with the farmer/landowner as a trade for services. Much of these transactions were by a Gentleman agreement often consisting of no more than a customary handshake between the gentleman farmer and the gentleman Gypsy. So often these strips of land were passed on from one generation of traveller to the next over many decades or even centuries.

Amongst us living here were a vast number of skilled artisans of all kinds. Including those of metal tin craft,smithery,brick makers,potters,horse and dog breeders,breeders of birds such as miners,menders of furniture,sharpeners of tools,fairgrounds and show people,pugilist boxers,bike riders,flower girls,tellers of fortune, scrap dealers and general labourers. The area boasted not only a strong history with famed smugglers such as Gulliver the landlord living in his lodge in Kinson at East Howe lane just a stone throw away. Whilst the Pelhams house in Millhams lane in the village itself stood majestically nearby with its spacious gardens and majestic trees and nearby village school and chapel. Along with the 11th century St Andrews church at the end of church lane. Where it was oft-times said that smugglers hid their contraband and where a tea smuggler is buried. Alongside so many of our people . Of course there were others in the Parish where our folki were baptised,wed n buried including at St Marks in Talbot Wallisdown and in Newtowns St Clements. In Kinson at the rear of the St Andrews church was a small estuary of the river Stour which sported a wooden bridge used by the many visitors to the Canford Magnas lodge home of the aristocratic Lord and lady Cornelia of Wimbornes Guest family. There were other bridges of bricks designed by the Guests to assist their regular visitors throughout the parish. There were many cottages scattered around the tree lined roads of the village. Including those fine distinctive pretty red bricked cottages built courtesy of Lady Wimborne to house the working poor. These were spread out throughout the kinson parish of Poole and Bournemouth. There were also many thatched cottages nearby at East Howe and a large white stoned house on church lane itself where travelling families the Crutchers, Jeff's and family lived there with their pig sties in the grounds. In the centre of the village was the village green where the local Revd. Sharp was busy with his young team of cricketers some of whom were chosen to play for England. The kinson village green was used for local events such as maypole dances on maypole days and here local criminals wrong doers from the locality were put in wooden stocks and local folk were able to throw rotten vegetables at them.

This was a time of high unemployment many families in Alderney and Newtown were very poor. Just a few miles away on the Wallis downs the Talbot family sisters who had visited the area as children were creating a community in the woodlands. Providing work for locals with housing for workers within a community of church, farm outhouses and a school for the children. The heathlands including Poole heath and Canford encompassed the community of Newtown at Parkstone in Poole. With acres of heather lands scattered over the land in which local Gypsy Travellers lived in their numerous encampments. At one time it seemed that the whole area was but a massive encampment. The area was rich in clay,gravel and sand which provided growing numbers of clay pits,sand and gravel pits, potteries and brickworks. Providing much needed work for local people with a great local natural sea port at hand at Poole. Here ships exported locally made exquisite pottery, bricks,tiles and other commodities which were renowned throughout the world. Poole had in earlier years been a highly profitable dock with its rich trade with Newfoundland. We had Turbary rights granted to us in 1248 which ended in 1822 with the Enclosure Act.

RYE FARM

(Photo courtesy of Kevin Crocker)

I walked to Rye farm upon top of Rye hill
where chickens did peck n ganders ran still
where goats they did chew from the leaves of the bush
and I sat down for breakfast with another wise mush
We ate fresh laid eggs and the bacon so good
the farmer he served me the best that he could
the turkeys were calling and the dogs they did yap
I ate of my toast spilled crumbs on my lap
the cows in the fields at the back of he sheds
the road it was busy with tanks full of lead
the countryside spread was a sight to be seen

just like Hardy wrote oh delightful of scenes
the farmer was Crocker the free loving man
he raced all the dogs at Poole racing stands
the walkers and tourists they often called
sat with the yokels the grockers and all
twas warm in the summer on top of rye hill
where the farm it was rich in manure smell still
where the poets told stories and of Cyril Wood fame
from the village of Bere and top of Butt lane
there was Bloxworth and Shitterton too
just down the track where wanders the fools
the Barnes built the houses and the village was famed
with its tales of the back woods and the fairground that came
but the farm has its place in the halls of the famed

Ray Wills

Upon Rye hilltop

On hill of Rye Upon Bere Regis walk
there was no need for idle talk
where village volk did stop n stare
all crowded leas and cattle bare
where stream did flow n boughs did bend
where daisies spread and men lament
I took a stroll oer donkeys lane
n wrote a poem near to the wain
where Barnes n Hardy wrote with pen
fashioned verse to pleasure men
where damsels strolled upon hill and brow
where zunners run and fields of cows
frisked their tails and mooed the days
where flies did taint their udders swayed
the farmer Crocker laughed and sighed
next to the road where tanks did ride
his dogs did yap and hens did peck
upon the corn and grit inspect
the bells did chime from high church tower
whilst young boys hid upon the bowers
the village life it hums and strolls
I watch the sky for signs of crows
my verse it haunts the sacred village scene
Amongst the hills and meadows young mans wishes
and old mens dreams

Ray Wills

UPON WOODBURY HILL-BERE REGIS

Once Gypsies camped on Woodbury hill
it were the home of fairs and folks remember it still
with fortune telling booths n village gals
ole in the tooth along with blacksmiths tending hooves
where Hardy penned and folks did boast
he shot at the famous fairground galleries most
vor as Hardy said "Bere it twere a blinkerin place"
where thousands came to this kingly place
since way back in the 12th century
they sold ponies there and gathered zum
on the hill of Hardys green afore the sun
there were thin men n fat uns n ladies too
miles away from the port of Poole

two headed calves,dancers and performers alike
locals charged for grokels to park their bikes
with coconut shies and nine pin stalls
lots of fun vor girl and boy
Twas held each September for a week
where volks did travel across from Dorchester streets
As well as faraway places such as Brum,Bristol Exeter and also
all their Cockney chums
with oyster day and penny day too
it boasted it was the biggest in the south
those days be gone and the hill still stands
so proud with woodland copses and green pleasant grounds
lording over this little town

Ray Wills

A walk on Turbary

The Smugglers Wain-Artist David Harbott as pictured at the rear of the Hub library Kinson

I went a walking on Turbary heaths
where Dartford Warblers did tweet on peat
I crossed the sandy paths where Gypsies meet
where little chavvies cut their teeth
Not that far from Wally Wack
Kinson Mead and old Gullivers deeds and back
where Augustus John painted the scenes
of young girls hopes and young mens dreams
the winding tracks through heather bounds
where a Phillips grazed his horses pounds
whilst Longham bridge did haunts our minds
by lady Wimborne cottages where roads did wind

the hills of lodge and Magna lane
where once stood brickyards and makers then
the winding sandy tracks and zen
wishing with my pen to go back to those times again

Ray Wills

Lavendar Fields

Lavendar Fields at Corfe Mullen courtesy of Sally Slocombe

They worked out in the Corfe Mullens lavendar fields with the
lavender,lilac and the downs
where acres of plantations spread
and baskets full were shared around
they took them to the factory and perfume sets were fayred
then sent them on the good railways the nation to be proud
Favoured by the Victorian Queen and her aristocratic friends
and maids the workers worked the fields and lanes the Gypsies
and the crew
through Corfe Mullen, Broadstone and Upton in Poole

Ray Wills

How soon we forget

Upton Brick works Poole

How soon we forget
the brickyards and clay
the pipes that they smoked
the light of the day
how soon we forget the wheels as they roll along
the Gypsy man and the Gypsy man song
how soon we forget who worked the land
the potteries and chimneys
the old Gypsy tan
who tended the land and worked on the clay

built all the bricks in those olden days
how soon we forget
the lavender fields where Gypsy gals gathered
the best of the crop
sold flowers in Bournemouth square
in baskets full tops
how soon we forget and cast them aside
turn out their trailers and waved them goodbye
how soon we install the ole trespass laws
the Lord of the manor dawns here once more
and the Gypsy Gals songs not heard no more

Ray Wills

Donkeys lane

Art picture courtesy of Dawn Jeanette Grant Harrison

We rode our wagons down the donkeys lane
afore the motor car got the blame
we travelled high to hill of Rye
picked some Bramley apples for our pie
the ground was wet with dew
mushrooms were out and i loved you
the farmers land was rich and proud
the meadows stretched across the hills just like a shroud
We travelled across to visit Wool
trains were in the station heading for Poole
the station masters name was Tom

he kept chickens at the rear n reared em young
he smoked a pipe with baccy strong
Wool bridge manor house had a ghost
a white lady in a carriage Im told
our wagon wheels they rolled along
we told our tales sang our songs
we took the road to Wareham town
fine granary with corn sold by the crown
When master Barnes was young and fancy free
Long afore Hardy wrote tales of all the country leas

Ray Wills

In Barnes Day

When Barnes did write of Linden
Lee
There were girt trees with bowers wide and boughs ung free
Ee wrote of Durzet dialect n history in the finest of poetry
Where wild flowers grew on lawns n banks n tuffs of grass and
zunners danced
In Hardys country where volks did chance to view the scenes of
young lambs skip n dance
Counting the hours to evenings tide sea-saw games of future
brides
Where church bells rang n town clock chimed n vicars prayed
Volks would gather on village green to celebrate the maypoles
Queens parade
Whilst ganders n ducks ran and zunners played amongst the
stacks of hay
When a Sovereign was richer by far than half a crown
Volks did gather round in Dorchester town
Barnes was Mayor and master teacher priest n Mathamatican
too
He wore long white gown n buckled shoes
Barnes did pen such fine poems with his Durzet tomes
Amongst the fields were fox n rabbits roamed
he couldnt abide the rich farm volks who took the poor mens
taxes and oats
Where Maidens Castle stood without tower or moat and volks
were poor without a vote
Where villagers green n farming land was set aside in their
masters plans
Where old maids prayed vor young uns

health and courting couples laid upon the grass
Where volks did know their place and toff their caps to gaffers
rich like gentry squires
Amongst the views of Purbeck hills where gaffers rode on
stallions rich
oer pastures commons and dirty ditch
His statue now stands proud in the Dorchester town
Whilst modern life rolls along
with its busy streets of pedestrians
whilst traffic flows and lights do bleep
and tourists walk its hills n streets
Barnes looks on without a peep
the master poet looks on down upon the volks of his old town

Ray Wills

Gypsy Childhood

The author as a child on the Mannings heath which is now Tower Park

My aunt Mary Mabey made the flower wreaths and flowers for the shows
Aunt Maisie Castle read the tea leaves then
it seems so long ago
Uncle Bill Rogers he told the stories and yarns fit for a king
My Granfer Reg made the bricks back then
My great Aunt King was a Gypsy Queen

My great gran Emily was a lady she wore her Fancy clothes
they made a roads name after her
it was so long ago
my long time granfer Jim Hansford was a strong man
he lived upon the moors
my cousin Jean was a dancer
the Queen of Poole carnival show
my cousin George was a choir boy and school organ maker too
my uncle Sid rode n the Monte Carlo Rally
my aunt Vera was a Dominey
she lived in one of granfers houses
he had many from Newtown to Alderney
my great uncle Harry was a house builder by trade
my father was a romantic he wrote letters and played the darts
he was a fine tree surgeon nearly fell to his grave
My Mother served the military and waited on great folks at
Wareham
He was Billy Wright the captain of the land he played soccer
and married Joy Beverley with his one hundred caps in hand
our landlord was old Cedric Hughes his mother was a Gypsy
Queen
the artist John Augustus at Alderney Manor painted our house
known as heather view
before we all lived on the Mannings Heath with a lovely view
of Poole

Ray Wills

Horace Cooper

Old Horace Cooper was a good friend of mine
he could tell you a yarn and spin you a line
when he lived on the heathland Annie and he
in old Wallisdown just a stones throw from me
he would lean on his gate and talk with the kids
carve out his script on the branch of a tree

in those days of the brick yards in old Alderney
we were the cousins of the Castles and friends of the Kings
the Whites were our histories with Stanleys thrown in
Mary and Maisie made flowers so grand
all the wreaths and the baskets from their tender hands
Ole Horace has a picture it hung on the wall
the storytellers of history its traditions and lores
just by the ditch was their home in old Wallidown
where the gypsies did roam not far from Poole town
it was the haunts of the smugglers and pens of the free
Augustus Johns painting all sketched in old Alderney
where the goldfinch did sing upon the thistles and
broomstickwhere the heathers were rich and the gypsies all
sung by the light of the moon
many did live there in cackers canyon Arne Avenue
the Johnstons and Mabeys and Joker from Poole
old Horace was rich but poor in he hand
but he had the true ways of the travelling man
he rode a good cart wagon through Wallisdown
he waved and smiles at the ladies on his drive to Poole town.

Ray Wills

ROMA MAN

He was a genuine Travelling Roma
horses were his life
he lived on the heath and commons
worked the land with his lovely buxsom wife
he was one of the old school Gypsy
who rode the lanes and dells
his family lived in benders then
afore the masters tales
he was a genuine Roma
with heritage which went way back
twas when they worked the brick yards
sacking on their backs
he was a genuine Roma
his sisters worked the fields
baskets full of lavender
lots of floral goods
his mother went a Duckerin
knocking on folks doors
his aunt she read the tea leaves
scrubbed the masters great hall floors
his father was a brick maker craftsman of the old
the chavvies ran the dog pack
were happy boys n girls

Ray Wills

SHOWMEN DAYS

My fathers was a showman
a Gypsy King by trade
a king of the circus and fairgrounds parade
my mothers a teller of fortune and seers
my brothers kept ponies over the years
my sisters are dancers
the Queens of the shows
in the family histories of long tImes ago
the chavvies grew strong
whilst us mushes were free
travelling the country
telling the stories of diddle dee dee
My folks worked the land and the fairgrounds parade
built swing boats and caravans
danced with the blades
we lived by our trades
our destiny proud
our ways they were strange
to the city brigade
we played on our drums and accordians too
from Mitcham to Brighton
Blackpool to Glasgow
then Penzance to Poole

Ray Wills

THE GYPSY CAMP

Art Picture courtesy of Dawn Jeanette Grant Harrison

He grew upon the Gypsy camp
with mushes proud and where pretty gals did dance
where vardos stood so tall n proud
near benders bush and music loud
where heathers grew upon the floor
no strangers came knocking at their door
where folks did sit around the yog
at night the stories told amidst the yapping of the dogs
where rabbits ran down country lanes
whilst foxes watched their daring games
he ran with chavvies barefoot too

with ferrets free in pockets deep
whilst ole ladies did a duckerrin do
where horses gables iron shod shoes
n babes did sleep amongst the dew
where lavender fields with baskets rich
did grace the views and commons ditch
so rich were the days and night time shades
when folks and dreamers had it made
amongst the poets dreams and shades
we graced the earth and set the scenes
where only modern folks do dream

Ray Wills

Fairground Tales

Art picture courtesy of Dawn Jeanette Grant Harrison

She read it in his tea leaves
before the starlight show
there beneath the canopy
the wonder fairground show
he heard her words of mystery
Gypsies cannot lie
she read it in his palm that night
before the crowds went by
the sounds of the Childrens laughter
the loud melodic rock
Bill Haley and the comets
Elvis and the rolling stones
now Gypsies cannot lie
she looked into her crystal ball
looked into his eyes
her scarf and golden earrings
her rings and tattoed arm
used all her Gypsy charm
he wondered how she knew so much
it could not all be lies
she promised love and fortune soon
a lovely summer bride
he was transformed by her ways
her intuition and her styles
she read it in the night time skies
within the wondrous show
a fairground rich in wonders
she was a Gypsy wonder show

Ray Wills

The Travelling Mush

I travelled down the highways
down those Gypsy lanes
talked with Squires and farmers
pat the horses mane
I strolled across the meadows
to the Gypsy site
the blossoms were a buzzing
the sun was high in sky
we sat around the yog that night
we talked just you and i
the stories that we shared that night
of times so long ago
fairground Gypsy boxers
the winds the frost the snow
the mushes that we knew and loved
the Gypsy girl and i
the lovers that we hugged loved n more
the fishes in the streams
the lost horizons in the mist
the long forgotten dreams
the shadows and the sunsets
the chavvies running free
the lovers on the meadows sweet
all past histories
yet seemed so real to me
the thunder storms and rainfall sweet
the horses and the rides
the fairgrounds and the weddings
the suitors and the brides

the vardo wheels a turning
the wheelwrights coopers frames
the Stanleys with the handsome bricks
the chaffinch down the lanes
the running brooks and meadows
the haystack where we lay
sweet corn rising on the distance I hear a baby born
welcome to the morn

Ray Wills

GYPSY FAIR

Art picture courtesy of Dawn Jeanette Grant Harrison

He met her at the Gypsy fair
whilst the old accordion played
he looked into her eyes and soon he was her slave
she whispered words of eloquence and offered him her charms
he took her to the waltzer ride and she melted in his arms
the stars were shining bright that night and the crowds were all
in tow
her dress was rich with satin silk and with rings upon her toes
he loved the way she moved that night n blessed her finest
clothes
she told him lies and offered alms yet he was lost to love

he took her by her words and prayers and the night was young
and gay
they spent that night together until the morning light
then she was gone forever like God turned out the light

Ray Wills

Brick Maker

Reg Rogers family friends and neighbours

My Granfer was a brick maker
he worked the kilns and downs
life was hard amongst the shifts
working for a crown
the landed gentry owned the land
whilst the common people prayed
the Gypsies worked the pits and clay
all the land around
the vardos and the benders
the huts with wagons strong
the chavvies running through the mire
with sweet lavender growing wild
the hours were long in brickyards then

when families were close
the donkeys and the ponies
the bricks sailed from the coast
my Granfer was a brick maker
his family owned the yards
red bricks to build the Bournemouth town
with sand pits closely by
they worked the kilns and clay pits then
with Gypsies standing by

Ray Wills

ROYAL BLOOD ROMA

Betty Blue Smith *Packman Billington in a scene from the film*
GHOST GYPSY

They say she had royal blood running in her veins
they said she was born on the heath one Saturday
they say she was true Romani bred
she picked the flowers she made the beds
she lived in a vardo gayly painted wooden van n sheds
fancy lamps and brassy urns tall stories in the morn
they said she was rich in dreams and fortune telling games
she planted herbs and knew all their fancy latin names
they say she grew up rich in tales and fancy rhymes
sing us a song Roma tell us a rhyme
They said her parents were Dominey n Sherwood bred

teachers of the pulpit flowers in the shed
her brothers and her sisters worked the farmers lands
hops and fruit give me your hands
the heaths were rich and the fields were free
stopping places, Atchen Tans such a history
write it down

Ray Wills

Romani boys

I am no Dominic Reeves Ive got no Gypsy story up my sleeve
I know Augustus knew Picasso
he was a true Gypsy Romani
though Augustus was just a bohemian
long before the Queen wrote rhapsody
Im no transcript writer of eloquence
no performer of great deeds
Im not a tight rope walker
like Elvis i believe
he was a Gypsy pelvis crooner
before hip hop was the sound
they played the Gypsy violins to the masses in the crowds
the vardos vans were awesome and the coopers knew the Kings
the fairgrounds were the places to be
on an autumn Saturday come see
the tattooed lady and the bearded friends
the python and the crew
the music played on the carousel
and the darts flew flights and more
the card sharp player had the best hand
the Gypsy Queen she once did dance
when the wall ride of death drew in the crowds and the famous
boxing booths
the heathlands and the heathers with lizards in the sun
the Gallows hill and the history
go tell it more my son

Ray Wills

STOPPING PLACES

Art picture courtesy of Dawn Jeanette Grant Harrison

I recall our stopping places and the many atchen tans way out in
the waste lands where the wind did chill our hands winters they
were lonesome we tended to stay free hidden in the woodlands
of this great forestry
I remember all the folki why they could tell a say sitting round
the yog at night the horses chewing hay the chavvies tucked in
their beds and the babes fast asleep
their mothers bedtime stories they sometimes took a peep
way out in the country down some old Gypsy lane where the
masons cut the stones by day and the rabbits ran the lanes

where the blossoms shed their perfumes and the gorse did catch
your toes
way out in the country lanes
there the places i loved most
all those stopping places where the old uns tell their yarns
where the queen of Gypsies honoured us with her tales and old
dam songs
where the gaffers were a sleeping in their mansions and their
farms
whilst we were out a roving the hillsides and the lanes where
songbirds were our music and the fires shed their flames

Ray Wills

THE BRICKWORKS OF NEWTOWN

There were scores of Inns in old Poole town
where bricks were made for king and crown
with yards and breweries and potteries too
they made a fortune for the lords of Poole
the brick makers and potters worked from dawn to dusk
to gain a living and earn a crust
they worked the kilns and brickyards hot
fathers mothers children the lot
their wages paid in all the retreats and lodge
they drank the liquor and the law did dodge
the clay was hot and heavy loads
the kilns were many and the sweat they groaned
there were scores of Inns in old Poole town
With Fancy dames with their fancy gowns
the coppers caught the drunken slobs
put them in the clink and money robbed
the Gypsy brick makers and the local yobs
all worked the kilns and the potters clay
long long hours to earn their pay
the bricks made the Bournemouth town
the landed gentry estates and their London homes
the Gypsy slept upon the downs
some in the brickyards far from the town
then when the work was not in demand
the Gypsy Travellers worked the land
in autumn they worked Poole fairground booths and stalls
strong men fighters dare devil riders and pretty girls
they went Dunkerrin their fortune skills
from fairground frolics to Canfords lodge hills

lavender flowers and herbs to save
the health of the nation
home of the brave

Ray Wills

WAREHAM TOWN DAYS

In Wareham town long time ago
the winters were bad we had deep snow
the river was frozen n we skated there
then in summer times there was a fair
there was Jackie Lock n Sue Anderson too
Cedric Hughes he rang the bells
at Lady St Marys he could tell a tale
Chalkie White and Younger Dave
Michael Joseph the one legged Romeo
the Beverly sisters and Billy Wright
at the black bear hotel they spent the night
young David Mellors dad taught at the school
there were saw pits and sand pits too

you could catch the train to Swanage and Poole
Les Hurst was the station master
he worked at Carey camp
cooked the meals there all the kids took a chance
on Saturday at corn exchange we held a dance
ken Samways lived by the walls
where the farm was neat beneath the trees
we fished for minnows on the quay
n walked to ridge and Redcliffes leas

Ray Wills

On Canford Magna road

We drove to Canford Magna road with rhododendron's on the
way
the lane was steep and pastures wide hadn't been there for don't
know when
we passed the school where kids did play and cuckoos chirped
each day
out by the Merley waste about where the houses spread their
way
on village life was quiet then in days of Lady Wimbornes time

where zunners knew their place where toffs were mean and lads
were lean
where farmers worked the land whilst bees did buzz amongst
the fuzz
whilst children played their games down such country lanes
the cottages were declared with thorns of roses red and white
the bricks were red where poets led their dreams into the night
the cottage thatched and tall green grass with narrow lanes to
walk
the talk was proud where willows bowed and chestnuts fell to
ground
whilst gypsy crew from here to Poole made flowers fit for
shrouds
the meadows sweet with berries to eat and daisies at your feet
where folks did pray and some did say that church is where
you'll meet
the school still stands within those grounds and the village
sleeps for sure
saved by the plans of wisdom's man though rabbits run for
cover true
far from the shores of Bournemouth core just a journey up from
Poole
the birds do sing there from winters to spring and summers play
the tune
where lady did live and heart did give to bless the peoples core
the likes of her we'll see no more yet the village speaks its all
the Dorset bricks and common tricks of poets steeped in grace
cannot explain the heritage fame of guests that once did preach
the rights of man to understand the beauty of this place

Ray Wills

Dominic Reeves

Dominic came to Kinson downs where Gypsies bedded and all
young girls were heaven bound
the vardo wheels did turn there and times were tough on the
common land of peat and bluff
he road the trails of bracken down where birds did sing o'er
rabbits mounds
where folks worked hard when hours were long amidst the days
of swallow song
where Mountbatten arms doth stand today afore shoulder of
mutton along the way
where birch did grow amidst heathers sweet with adder n
lizards at your feet
near Alderney where Augustus John did paint naked ladies so
frequent
where Sankey Ward built houses for the rich and lady
Wimbornes lodge was close to pitch
the writer stored his memories of gypsy life neath sky and trees
where crafts were rich in lore and pen where kids grew tall and
fern did bend
the local people in Kinson free where rich in style and histories
the Longham bridge over the Stour to Ferndowns haunts and
village squires
the war had took the youth its true with tales of valor from
Waterloo
the commons rich in gravel clay and stone but to the Gypsy it
was home
where grass was mean and trails were sand and fortunes told to
open hands

where families came from New forest glades to build their
homes n get it made
Dominic wrote and his wife did paint the gypsy story oh so
quaint
till they were all housed on West Howe land with bricks of
Rogers builders band
the chimneys grew tall upon the land and pigs were sold in
markets grand
the gaffers paid you on the land and the rich grew richer you
understand
those days of Gypsy life so free were recorded there in histories
with Dominics books of fame and lore he painted it as it was
after the war
the Gypsy families are still abroad you can hear them sing with
one accord
their heather sprigs are sold today in Poole high street just like
twas yesterday

Ray Wills

Those were the days of Gypsy lore

Photo from GHOST GYPSY

Those were the days of Gypsy lore no idle hands to feed the
poor
there were stopping places here n there making bricks mending
rocking chairs
days and nights November there were ole Poole fair lots of
chavvies nippers all went there
there were folks who knew you with quirky names the Kings n
Castles, Lees n James
quirky places uncle toms on the commons we got along
up on hill n Wally Wack benders vardos tents n sacks
cuckoo bottom n Corfe Mullen ridge, heavenly bottom, Rogers
Sids

crooks n tallys deals and more, Wally Cave Johnny Turner and
Ronnie Moore
Freddie Mills the boxing king Ted Sherwood and Charlie King
up Sea view and down the Poole lane to pub shoulder and
mutton with the family James.

Rogers he did make the bricks with Brixeys n Mabeys and the
dam little midge
Lady Wimborne and her cottages n bridge
run and roll of the dice and flower gals in the square
Augustus John, Grace Clapcott too, Emily Fancy and ladies
bare
those were the days of long time past when dreams were made
and curse was cast
when Gypsy travellers roamed the lanes of old lodge hills and
the Stours pane
where Longham bridge did mighty roar and the saw pits
Rossmoore and the brickyard chimneys soared high
where once rabbits ran free and foxes too
from all of Canford Magna n across to Waterloo

Ray Wills

Candles in the dark

Nights spent in the fairgrounds
Poole park rides on the train
walks down Sea View
constitutional hills, the wind and the rain
days spent in the playground
tarmac surfaces frozen ice
miniature bottle milk with straws
candles to bed at night
coney gatherings on the commons
motor bikes speedway stars
camp building on the heather
Gypsies at Woolworths

gatherings around yogs see the sparks
conkers and marbles flick cards and more
teachers slates and ink wells
come in for tea mother calls
candle in the dark at bedtime
uncle macs radio
bedtime stories of the seven
listen to the dogs bark
friends and neighbours
chasing rainbows flying kites
blessings on Sundays
trip to the park

Ray Wills

Gypsy days and night

George Castle and John Dove at the Mannings

Working at the forge with Reuben and George
sitting around the yog got my handle and my cards
telling tales of long ago says and wonders drinking slo
chavvies and babes tales of olden time slaves
kingdom and little Egypt home

royal blood horses cobs n shetland prime
forest days shows and fairs
the carousel turns and the jukey plays
blue skies and starry nights
wind of change fortunes told and fine wreaths made
flower girls and cousin Marys dance
lots of mushes and evil eyes
New England, Heather lands and old gals wise
Kings and Queens tins and pans
sing us another song Gypsy man

Ray Wills

TRAVELLERS LAMENT

Art picture courtesy of Dawn Jeanette Grant Harrison

She took a reading he worked the forge she collected flowers
she mixed the herbs
he bred the horses and mules a few full of birdsong on the
heaths of Poole
He worked the fairgrounds she flew the darts he rode the cars
starlight in the dark
She cooked the stew he told the tales the land was rich wagons
and tails

He shook the hands and bartered deals she picked the fruit turn
turn turn wagon wheels
they used the stopping places and atchen tans he told the stories
he was the man wise old ways gypsy man She stood for
Munnings pictured frames Stanleys, Lees, Coopers,James the
same
She dressed in skirts and gay bright rings he wore the waistcoat
sports of kings
She fashioned flowers paper crepe he worked with clay gravel
and bricks
She sang the songs of Caroline Hughes he wrote the stories
Dominic Reeves
She modelled for John at Alderney he built the cottages Lady
Wimborne free
She danced at pubs in forest glades he collected iron scrap She
was Queen thousands at her grave
he was a scholar poet bard she was a countess he played the
cards
she was a sweetheart of Byron too he was a wanderer traveller
from Poole
He was a boxer the sport of Kings
he was Ted Sherwood preacher and fairground King
she was a Kinson coal merchant and he was a king
she was a Cole he was a White where gold finch did sing into
the night.
She was a dreamer he was a priest she saved lives he saved
souls to teach
she was a beauty and he was a rogue she was a prophet he was
a fool they rode their wagons through the streets of Poole

Ray Wills

56

LIVING IN NEW ENGLAND

Nancy Crutcher at Millhams lane Kinson

Im living in New England by the Fernheath valley spruce
where the heather and the brambles roam across the paths aloof
im walking down the same ole tracks where once the folki
roamed
where the Dartford Warbler still doth sing and the sand lizards
have their home
Im sat here reminiscing of how things used to be
when the travellers lived upon the heath not far from Alderney
where the peat they cut in turves so clean and the blackberry
was rich
close by the birch and ferns where they paddled in the ditch
The Longham walk was rich and free and the Stour was rushing
oer
where the waterworks gave out its roar and the ponies bridled
poor
where the rich man and the poor man said prayers they bought
their floral wreaths from Nancy at Millhams lane
where the old old church still stands seems so far away
The gorse was thick and noble and the fuzz was rich in
perfumed flower
where they lived upon the common then and sold heather n
flowers
where their baskets were so awesome and the town it clock did
chime
where Jeffs and Whites were settled in the land of Gypsy
rhyme.

Ray Wills

COY MEADOWS

On Bourne valley walk
the flowers were in bloom
Irises, lillies scented perfumes
Rhododendron bushes so mixed to delight
willow trees shady
foliage so light
Greens and the browns
red and the blues
water streams rushing
light of the moon
Bridges of Iraq
Victorian stream
water tower of brick
Durrant families dream
Fountain so perfect
walks to delight
meadows of coy
to please girl n boy
both day n night
Landscaped of beauty
grass and wood planks
walkways and benches
sun blessed delights
Folks out a walking
girl on a bike
dogs on a lead
poetry read

oh what a pleasure
this heavenly bed

Ray Wills

SWANAGE

The hills of Swanage stand steep and proud
with Purbeck stoned dwellings
quaint little lodge homes
tall scenic remnants of a bye gone age
far off the highway
the home of the sage
Twisted roads weary with hedgerows in tow
sandy beaches that stretch
seagulls and crows
little thatched cottages
quaint hotel retreats
tidy shop fronts with gifts well in reach
Sandy beach avenues with freedom to run
summer kissed meadows
a place in the sun
high in the distance
the castle on the hill
brambled highways
views that could kill
Long country walks
cute little lanes
a place to retire to
or come back again

Ray Wills

Newtown CHILDHOOD DAYS

Charlie Eaton brought the pig swill from the finest hotels in the
land
Sankey Moody chopped the finest meat at his butcher home
delivered to your door
Mary Mabey made the finest floral wreaths and fine displays
to celebrate your romance and your lovely wedding day
We all shopped at up on hill Us kids all attended the Regal
cinemas matinees each Saturday
Rogers was the warden at the St Clements church
he ushered folks out before the service ended he was so alert
the fairground was at the Branksome rec each holiday
twas where we spent our pennies n passed our youth away
consti was our sea view we could look through the periscope
that day
view Poole harbour and the Purbeck hills many miles away
We took our accumulator batteries to be charged at Rossmore
so as we could listen to Dick Barton special agent and Journey
into space too
Bill Knott son of a Gypsy made the caravans and took them on
the roads
Ryvita crispbread factory just across the lane
where the Gypsy Queen Caroline Hughes parked up with the
Warrens, Turners and Kings
where Abe Stanley became the local boxing king
Waterman chased us on his bike at Branksome heath school
then if we did not attend

Ray Wills

ROSSMORE DAYS

Photo of Reginald Rogers known as Bill Rogers courtesy of Lynda Stuchberry

We lived in our house wagons upon the Pembrooke road
there were lots of Gypsy families there like Hopes and James
and even Nellie Old
they parked upon their old grandmas yard they said they were
as good as gold
least that is the story Ive been told
there were lots of Gypsy folks in the Rossmoor hotel and a saw
mill down the road
the Circus ringmaster he had a whip and the chavvies they all
laughed when ole Stanley spit
we had a lot of fun those days n bathed in old tin baths
there were quarries on the commons then and lots of rabbit pies
the Kings and Warrens ran the lanes and there was a stream a
running bye
We lived in our house wagons off of the Rossmore roads
there were lots of nappos and divvies around us then and a co
op divi too along with newts n toads
we caught the bus to Up on Hill and walked to see the Regal
flicks
there were lots of friendly neighbours then we had our penny
bicycles and no one had a quid
but we were happy on the heath then playing with our dustbin
lids
the Sherwoods they were boxers and where the Cacker Canyons
Arne Avenues Hurdy Gurdy man played
close by the Gypsy campsites with little Wally Cave, the
Brixeys and the Rogers, Smalls,Phillips folks and Trent
We had accumulator radios and lavender perfume scents
the gal's they had their baskets of flowers for to sell
there were our horses on the heaths then and turves with lots of
peat as well
our chavvies were well behaved though no shoes upon their feet

the school was down in Kinson village n another towards Up on hill whilst the Branksome Dartford warbler sang his song and the slo was in the still

Ray Wills

Brick makers of old Newtown

Tom Rogers with workers in Brixey road yard Newtown
courtesy of Steve Royce Rogers

There were scores of Inns in old Poole town
where bricks were made for King and crown
with yards and breweries and potteries too
they made a fortune for the lords of Poole
the brick makers and potters worked from dawn to dusk
to gain a living and earn a crust
they worked the kilns and brickyards hot
fathers mothers children the lot
their wages paid in all the retreats and lodge
they drank the liquor and the law did dodge

the clay was hot and heavy loads
the kilns were many and the sweat they groaned
there were scores of Inns in olde Poole town
fancy dames and fancy gowns
the coppers caught the drunken slobs
put them in the clink and money robbed
the Gypsy brick makers and the local yobs
all worked the kilns and the potters clay
long long hours to earn their pay
the bricks made the Bournemouth town
the landed gentry estates and their London homes
the Gypsy slept upon the downs
some in the brickyards far from the town
then when the work was not in demand
the Gypsy Travellers worked the land
in autumn they worked Poole fairground booths and stalls
strong men fighters dare devil riders and pretty girls
they went dunkkerin to fortune skills
from fairground frolics to Canfords lodge hills
lavender flowers and herbs to save
the health of the nation
home of the brave

Ray Wills

Purbeck

Have you been to Puddle town
Piddle Trent hide and Wareham town
have you strolled up Rye hill in Bere Regis
where the farm chickens peck and the views are a thrill
close by Shittington dont say it loud
the Norman church where they still wear shrouds
have you been to Binden hall old Creech Grange and Wareham
mill
have you strolled through Arne and seen the view
the harbour lights of port of Poole
have you heard about the ghost of Durberville Wool bridge
the Corfe Castle dungeons where Enid Blyton hid in Swanage
lived

have you been on the top of Warehams grassy walls
inside St Martins church at Warehams town seen the Lawrence
effigy and more
where once the ruler wore a crown
have you walked the Purbeck twisty lanes
the dips and dales
the views to kill
Have you lived the Purbeck life and walked the Purbeck hills

Ray Wills

The Square and the Compass

On top of the Purbeck where the stone was cold and mean
the travellers and hikers walked the paths of Dorset scenes
where yeomen once were local and the landed Gentry dwelled
where sheep and hills were rich in rhyme and the poets write
there still
in the olde stoned pub relic where fire sparked so free
where hearth is home to wanderers and folks who are free like
me
where Augustus John the artist pics were hung upon the wall
next to the old Stone museum where dinosaurs once roared
the masons etched their histories and the hills were rich in dew
where the wind blew cold on winter days deep within the hues

the dogs they sat down close to the fire and the drinkers toasted
zen
whilst olden Dorset folki breathed life into its flames
the sign it swung outside the pub where chickens all ran free
where stone tables laid their stories yet to see
the atmosphere was rich in trust and the poet viewed the scenes
upon the Purbeck hillsides there so close to Halloween
the square and compass told its tales upon the hilly downs
where lovers met and couples kissed their steps left far behind
the cockerel crowed and gave chase to the farmers wench
upon the Purbeck hillside where Hardy paid his rent

Ray Wills

Winfrith Village life

I went down to the village where the school yard it still stands
where children play in summertime and lovers all hold hands
I ambled down to poets lane and butts close nearby
where roses grew around the thatch and strangers all passed by
The post office was so quaint with doorbell that chimed
there was a village postman on his bike and a poet quoting
rhymes
the village church stood on a hill and a well was set in stone
lots of flowers on the paths and lots of quaint cute homes
The pigeons close was shelter there for sparrows all in line
with thrushes singing in the bush next to a washing line
the old school lane it beckoned me with its quaint rustic stone

where local yokels stopped to chat all on their own way home
The water lane was rich in grass with roses around each bend
where lovers stopped to kiss at night and old men would
pretend
the carpenters wee cottage was rustic and with charm
there were lots of dandelions on the banks and gypsies selling
alms
On giddy green the children played hopscotch and beggars fool
nearby the cob web cottage proud where nelson met his
Waterloo
the badgers brook was rich in life with poets passing through
just close to Wareham town n just a walk away from Wool
The rambling roses beckoned me and the banks were full of
flowers
every minute spent there was rich in countless hours
the sun smiled on the village scene and the church bell rang at
noon
when life was rich in village charm and it ended oh too soon -

Ray Wills

Judge Jeffries

Judge Jeffries was the hanging judge
he lived in Dorset town
with miles of open country
all belonging to the crown
with mark et day on Thursday
on Sundays there were hangings with everyone for free
for all the little children and family to see
Judge Jeffries was the hanging judge
he worked on Gallows hill
Bere Regis to Dorchester they remember him still
with miles of open country and nearby castle on the hill
there were Kings and Queens of England
who sat upon their thrones
where aristocracy was rampant
where common folks were poor
and wise men lived alone

Ray Wills

At Sugar Knob

Photo courtesy of Betty Smith Billington Packman

At Sugar Knob mountain
by monkeys hump lane
The Gypsies kept goats on long iron chains
In Cinders Town near Frying pan the chavvies danced where
rabbits ran
The Gypsies came to Wally Wack above High Moor
local folks had never seen their likes before
Their caravans vardos n wagons were decked with the finest of
lace
With polished glass n lamps for to show your face
There were so many Gypsy camps folks did say they travelled
from over France
Hemley bottom was the home of the fairground Kings

There were Sherwoods and Whites remembering
At Bribery Island folks did vote for Ladys boy
for to keep their homes n keep their quotes
For Lady Guest did free rent them out
to local lads to pay for their digger shag and baccy snout
They say they were upper class Gypsies that lived in Wolsey
road
The chavvies spinning tops were busy that side of the road
The rag Man Cooper came with wagon n heavy loads
At least there the stories he to me told.

Ray Wills

Such Majesty

We tided an tethered all our ponies and cobs with wagons
standing bye
next to Alders windswept lanes and bracken
whilst we drank within the Kings Arms
on the hillsides of Wallisdown
All its heavy iron rings were fastened to its wall
Where the wind blew oer the bracken
where the sisters Talbot built their village and the dwellings
for the poor downtrodden masses
in the time of John Augustus
in the days of Lady Cornelia Guest

Where the heather blessed the commons
and the Gypsies rode the lanes n blessed
The encampments on the common then were rich in stories n
true in faith
With all their chavvies running free
All their wisdom shared around their yog fires
All the virtues of the tribes
Ayres n Sherwoods, Coles and Stanleys, Jeffs and Coopers
Bless the bride,
sprigs of our heather for your luck dear
Off to Woolworths in Poole
Once we saw the dolphins ride upon the quayside there
Where the ships sail out to sea
Bound for to gain their fortunes in New Found lands
Rich in bounty in another time
Such Majesty

Ray Wills

Queen of the Castles and Kings

Art picture courtesy of Dawn Jeanette Grant Harrison

She was a Gypsy sweetheart
one time Queen of the Castles and Kings
She rode the Canford commons
she made the starlings sing
She was beautiful when she was young
she made the young men heads turn
she was a rare breed Gypsy girl
within the heathers and the thorns
She rode the caravans wagons of wood back then
When the wagon wheels did turn
She would dance and sing a melody
she made the young men yearn
then when she grew older
she lost her youthful good looks
her darkness held her furrowed lines of age
She made the children feel uneasy n disturbed
She was the Queen of the Gypsies
she died upon the Canford heath
she was buried in her wagons flames
Along with her belonging n her teeth

Her funeral was attended by hundreds of her clans
She was the Queen of the Gypsies mother of the Gypsy band
She was the Queen of the Castles and the Kings
the Newtown clans of Gypsy families
She grew up wise in tooth and wisdom
When I was a kid I remember she was so kind to me

Ray Wills

Augustus John and the Gypsies

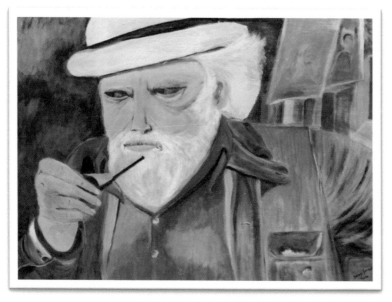

Art picture courtesy of Dawn Jeanette Grant Harrison

Folks say that Augustus was fascinated by gypsies
and that is why e drew n painted them every day
some in their fine and dandy clothes
some others naked in the hay
John was a roving bohemian guy
with his paint brush ready in his hand
he slept n lived upon the local common lands
with his vardo set in clay and dens
He at one time painted our Lady Wimborne rented house called
Heather View
with its pretty pink roses around its windows and door

with its red and its white bricks of the land
Where Crusoe came to call
They do say that Whistler the artist was a friend of his n Picasso he knew
Along with Lyodd George too
he sketched the Gypsy chavvies with local charcoal then
guess he knew Sid Rogers too
Now the famous London art museum stores his scenes to view
some are of the common Gypsy folki
others lost at sea in Poole
His wife was Ida and his sister Gwen
plus all his lovely maids lived within the manor road
close to locals like Wally Cave
His art studio there was made of glass
though his farm life was basic mean
for he kept lots of goats n pigs that he would wean
His looks were dark and foreboding n ugly then
with his long coat and his beard
folks said he was eccentric whilst others thought him weird
the art world though him a master stroke
with his flair for all things bright
he painted local girls in the nude in the naked light
but I guess he was alright

Ray Wills

Talbots two sisters

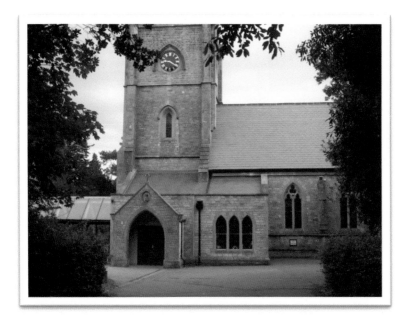

Where smugglers did haunt and poachers did prey
from the heathlands and commons of Canford
to the far off shores of Shell Bay
their boots they were worn and their children so poor
with lessons not learned and their manners absurd to the core
whilst the gentry were rich there and they owned of their lands
with houses so grand
but the poor labouring men were all not assured
Whilst the benevolent sisters they took up their cause
through the fine words of Owen and the cross of our lord
The village was crafted and those times they were drawn
with fine cottages built fit for the labouring weary and worn

with their stables and its farmland so free to transcend
with its community so rich in its peoples and blends
whilst fine primroses grew on its footpaths so true
With its fine church of St Marks
on the boundary of Bournemouth and Poole
where the Kinson estate stretched from Wimborne to the deep
bogs of old Waterloo
still rich in its folklore along wit the Gypsies and their
travelling crew
For the Talbots community was true to its cause
with the lords ten commandments and the decency laws
now the poor men were rich in their community life
By the strength of their hands and the skills of their knives
their school it was set there in the woods of the land
With its heathlands for grazing of cobs free for the fine Gypsy
bands
Close by the turbary commons n turf of the New England fame
the sisters had created a wealth within its stone gravelled lanes
There were sweet lodges so plentiful though local men knew
their place
where the squires were rich and men hid their face
in the woodlands n heaths where the rabbits ran free
this story of the Talbots is pure history
on the Wallisdown commons and in all its rich lanes
The folks grew their crops here once again whist the fox ran the
wain
once again the working man was free to gain the benefits of
open land once again
for the gaffers were dedicated and the land was free
where two sisters once pledged their trust in Thee

Ray Wills

Brownsea Island boys

Lady Baden Powell's own 1st Parkstone Scout Group at Delph Woods in 1946

I took a trip to Brownsea Island just a ride from olde Poole bay
where Baden Powell created the boy scouts movement one fine
day
there were just 10 public school boys
plus 10 lads from Poole town
he formed n led the first scout camp
at the cost of less than half a crown
on the island in earlier days was a hermit
in the 7th century
he lit fires then to warn sea men of the dangers and the perils
out to sea

In August they did celebrate the scouts 100 anniversary

I took a trip to Brownsea Island to see the pheasants on display
and the red squirrels scurrying freely
there were cockals in Poole bay
there were Sandbanks at Poole quayside
All the grockels are here to stay
with the boats out in the harbour
on such a lovely summers day
See the boy scouts camps on the island
all the zunners out to play

Ray Wills

.

Carey boy scouts

I once was a boy scout
at Carey schools camp
we put up our tents
and sang our camp songs
around campfires of logs
beneath pine trees so tall
and listened to sounds of wood pigeons call
We walked through the Purbeck
and Corfe in one day
we carried our rucksacks
full pack all the way
Then we had breakfast at the foot of the hill
Beneath the castle of Bankes
and I remember it still
We rode out to Brownsea
home of our clan
and had a nice red complexion
and a lovely dark tan
we did all the actions and sang all the songs
thats how we grew up healthy and strong

Ray Wills

The last knocker upper of Poole

Courtesy of Dorchester /Poole Museum

She was the last of the knocker uppers in the Dorset town of
Poole
Famous in the neighbourhood amongst the wise men and the
fools
her name was Caroline Cousins
known as the lady with the lantern n pole
everyone ones heard of her for Shes local dont you know
She was born in Morden village just outside of Poole
though she was not registered at birth
she was reared in a labourers cottage her life was not of worth
that was afore the first great war when she took up her role
of knocker upper around Poole quay
She was nicknamed Granny Cousins by the workers of the local
vines and potteries
She worked the dark streets six days a week
whether the weather was poor or fine
just to get them all up in time
She was always up well before the day broke with her bonnet
apron and shawl
you could always see her a shuffling down the narrow streets in
summers winters n fall
you would always hear her loud knocker upper call
It was when the ladies walking fields was called the Rose walk
folks in old Poole knew her well and you could hear them about
her talk
She became a salvationist when she retired
she was loved by the parish but she died penniless poor

Ray Wills

Roma Day

Photo Courtesy of Betty Smith Packman Billington

It was Roma Day in Dorchester town
Where Hardy penned and where Barnes did write his sweet
Durzet rich dialect poetry down
where the music from the accordions played
when Gypsies danced and dreams were made
The storytellers told their tales of the Dorset towns rich country dales
where farmers wives and dairy maids all gathered around
in the Dorset green rich country glades
they told their tales of days gone bye

when Caroline Hughes but but a child n shy
when the market town was rich in life
where yokels bartered dawn to night
where vardo wagons rolled and gypsies danced
across the hills like true romance
It was Roma day in Dorchester town
with happy folk all gathered around
where folks all came from miles around
for to share all their tales n fine displays
their vardos rich in fine attire
their chavvies in awe sat round the fire
they sung their songs of Gypsy rhymes
Sharing the brew of love divine
oh to hear the stories of travellers free
all the hopes and dreams of humanity
in Roma life
oh let it be

Ray Wills

The Gypsies flower girls dream

Photo courtesy of Betty Smith Packman Billington

Youl see them there on Saturdays
outside Bournemouth town great square
With baskets full of daffodils,lilacs and roses by the score
their braided hair and darker looks
with their dresses oh so gay
from heather sweet terrains they came
to while the hours away

Their dialect was course with melody
though their words were plain
they spoke the true Romani like children once again
they promised wealth good health and more
to people passing by
with smiles to warrant fortunes gained
with wisdom in their eyes
The homes of vardos on the heath and songs of yesterday
with accordions playing songs of love
with rabbits in the hay
with ponies small and dog juk packs calls
with heathers sweetly laid
amongst the hills where myxomatosis killed the food of
yesterday

Ray Wills

Vardo Days

Art picture courtesy of Dawn Jeanette Grant Harrison

I once had a vardo and its wheel thy did roll n spin
I rode it to Ringwood the great show in the spring
My father he boxed at the fairgrounds to the Lord Queensbury
rules
Oh the days they were long then when we lived down near
Poole

I once had a wife she was dark n so wise
she sang with the birds and had sparkling green eyes
she would tell folks their fortunes
so gorgas beware
dont you dare go pick all the heather from Pooles baskets fair
We worked in the meadows picking the hops and down at Poole
quay
for a many long hours our wages to see
We often drank beer outside the pubs by the sea
the lights they did shine there and the stars they were bright n
twinkled at night
Where the street light did glow
when we danced there at night whilst the old uns did sew
Though those days have long gone and the gaffers have too
Although I remember the days when we camped near sea view
there were cones on the hillsides and boats in the bay
Constitution hill was so steep and our lives were so gay
Our homes n our wagons were so rich then
decked out with satins and lace
with our tattoos and fancy artwork all over the place
our lamps they were gold and our talk it was free
when we lived by our wits for we were true Romani

Ray Wills

TREASURY OF DORSET

Art picture courtesy of Dawn Jeanette Grant Harrison

There is a treasury of Dorset
where true poets love to roam
streets lined with thatched cottages and lovely walks along the
river Frome
There is a coach and horses inn with a bear cross history
where Hardy wrote his novels for all like you and me
Theres a treasury awaits you there with a castle on a hill
where Purbeck stones are cut n crafted
amongst Purbeck meadows sweet and rivers flowing still
There was Barnes the master poet,teacher of the pen

where Bankes and Rogers crafted those histories of local
Quarry men
The treasury of Dorset awaits one every day
where pastures spread n daisies n folks were making hay
Theres the bird songs of the Turbary warblers
Whilst cannons still fired at dawn in Lulworth
Its where Blyton wrote of Noddy at Sandbanks
whilst grokel walkers spread the ferns
walks acoss the Egdon heaths to smell the scents of trees
Or wallow in the marsh n heathers of West Moors country
scenes
Where the spruce is growing tall and the deer trails are winding
free
for God is still in his heaven there and there are comforts in the
leas

Ray Wills

Old Poole Town

They knocked down our homes in old Poole town
old streets lights,washing gown,weathered storms
feathered beds with duck n down
washboard blues,tea chest refrain outside loos mothers birth
pains n old efrains
They made it rubble bricks n sticks n ole mens dicks,
they took away our fun n games ropes n skips hopscotch lanes
gone are the flea house flicks and alleyways
mothers calls and fathers ways
gone are the tears of yesterdays the Gypsy reels and the kiddies
play
the close knit families the old knocker ups and the holidays
along with the rag n bone man with his cart,
the gas lit streets where we did meet kissing n touching Mary in
the dark,

the ball games the gals all played upon the wall
knickers tucked, of Queeny king and bouncy balls,
mothers corsets ,fathers winter vests, chalk and cheese its
Sunday best
They demolished happy days and years of grace
with polished cardinal doorsteps n smiley see your face
They took way our alleyways where our dreams were all
displayed n made
they moved us all to Rossmoor place, Turlin Moor and wash
your face n know your place
Gone are the ways of old Poole town its boys n girls its ups n
downs.

Ray Wills

Dorset

I went fishing in Dorset and climbed the Purbeck hills
Swam in the sea off Studland and travelled so footloose
we camped in Carey on on the Corfe downs
Sketched the ruins of history and then went to old Poole Town

Nowhere can you find a place where each bends not the same
winding lanes of Purbeck stone and leafy heather lanes
where castle sits on hillside and boats are in the bay
where folks come from London and lands so far away
Dorset has its beauty the artist paints the scene
hardy wrote his tales of love and Blyton childish dreams
the hills are set in clay where stone of London's made

Gods in his glory and the meadows rich in glades

The Portland bill awaits you and the Durdle door it stands
where lulwoth bay is awesome and lovers all hold hands
the commons have their glory in Canford village scenes
one man writes its poetry and Barnes doth pen his dreams

The Wareham walls surround the town where kings were off
times gained
whilst Cromwell rode his armies and Bankes, Drax and Weld
did reign
all the ramblings of a poet cannot hide its wealth
where forests rich in fauna hide the deer and olden branch the
same

Ray Wills

Home at last

On walks with John we did frequent the roads of Wool where
zunners went
on Durburville green were crickets played and cavaliers band
made their plays again
where Winfrith sheds its mushroom lanes and the lion roars in
wind or rain
where ships hall once stood so old and grey welcomed the
troops whilst bands did play
The Wareham Worgret road and bridge the lanes that led to
Wool or Ridge
where chestnuts necked the boughs so mean whilst farmers
ploughed and young gals screamed

where young men took the weary tracks where brambles
blessed the cress fields sacks
where grooms did meet upon Wool green afore the church bells
rang and old Liz was queen
we walked the Purbeck hills once more my friend and i from
foreign shores
we shared our memories of Dorset bared where unions bands
were first declared
the Bere Regis headless women fame was nowt but tales of
Warehams reign
whilst Mellor and Master Stuckey trained the crew in manners
sweet and humble too
the Lawrence effigy doth declare that Shaw was rich in pastoral
care
that Egdon heath was wild and free where Hardy strolled and
Barnes drank tea
the hills they offered views to kill from Creech burrow top with
views of Poole
the Carey woods and Stoborough Green the yokels danced at
Halloween
so blessed were we to share these scenes from Bovingtons tanks
to Corfes great leans
where windy roads and stones are cast for wrens great work
were home at last

Ray Wills

Creech Days

We took a walk to Creech each year us kids from Wareham
town
we wore our best clothes Sunday best our smiles and girls in
gowns
we took a stroll to Creech burrow for picnic on the mount
each Easter hot cross bun day we did this our numbers you
could count

we climbed the hill to Dorset's scenes oh was a splendid site
with views of rivers hills and downs with fields all green and
bright
we talked and laughed and played those games that kids all like
to do

we could see across to puddle town and the power station at
Poole

there were birds that sang upon the downs where grass grew tall
and mean
with walks around the mount to top to view those splendid
scenes
the rabbits scrambled o'er the copse and foxes chased and
played
we could hear the lady st Marys bells and the chaffinch on the
trees
the days were long and sunny then with time to do just as you
please

there was hot cross buns with jam and pop which was sicking
and so cool
we tucked away our picnic there and looked across to Poole
the Somerset downs were prime and the Hampshire forest
moors
we could see the sea and smell the gorse and loved the
paddocked horse

us kids we strolled home weary and full of fun and mirth
across the Stoborough heath and woods to Wareham homeward
course
those days were full of memories and laughter with true grit
we talked and strolled that route each year where upon the
burrow wed sit

Ray Wills

Gulliver's Days

St Andrews church Kinson

Gulliver the pirate sailed in his Dolphins boat and pride
He Docked it in Poole Bay Chines when he was in his prime
Kinson was renowned for the famous splash at St Andrew's
church bridge
Where the green was rich in history of smuggling n that opened
up the lid

The roads were wide and open where Gypsies trails laid hid
amongst the Canford parish where treasure troves were hid
although the future king of Germany was saved by Kinson lads

now looking back on it they say they must have been so mad

In the grounds they buried old Trottman for stealing tea its true
He was wanted by the custom officers from Bournemouth down
to Poole
they say its all a sorry state that Gulliver ran the show
with pubs and property stretching from Ferndown his wealth
was sure to grow

Ray Wills

My Dorset

I wandered o'er these heath lands
Where the sun comes up each dawn
Where the rabbits run to greet you
Each and early morn

Where the meadows and the pastures
Are blessed by Gods own hands
Where the farmer and the tourists
Savour this sweet land

From Lyme to Christchurch Priory

Through Wareham with its mill
The effigy of T.E Lawrence
In the St Martins church upon the hill

The rivers Frome and Stour
The swans that sail on by
The pastures and the meadows
The birds up in the skies

there's a view to send you crazy
a scene to blow your mind
with hills of Maiden Castle
Creche Burrow you will find

The quay of Poole that flourished
In times of pirates bold
Where Gulliver sailed the waters
Contraband and Spanish gold

Woodes Rogers sailed to Newfoundland
With its cods, Ropes, hopes and dreams
Poole pottery it is famous
Like Dorset's haunting scenes

I strolled the hills of Purbeck
Saw that Portland stone
Which Wren used for London
And all those grand cellestrel homes

Here Hardy wrote his novels
Barnes penned poetry
Stevenson lived at Westbourne
With views out to the sea

There's views like Corfes Castle
With Rivers running free
Where the books of Enid Blyton
Came to life for me

Ray Wills

Wareham lad

As a lad I lived in Wareham town
where streets were narrow and church bells chimed
near the river Frome and Piddles rhymes
old Cedric Hughes did ring the bells
at lady St Marys church
all in good time
I shared those Sunday morning revelries
beneath Church's tower and willow trees

the village Romeo was one legged Mick
he rode a motor bike and sanctioned it
the village Stoborough had its green

where folks would gather from early spring till Halloween
the Miller mad did haunt the walls
where grass grew tall with tales of Roman lords

the tales were rich in history
and poets words of majesty
the cockerel crowed on Samways farm
to wake them up twas their alarm

the lizards squirmed on the high grass walls
where children played from each new dawn
the trumpet major rode this way
whilst Hardy wrote and lambs did play

the poet William Barnes lived just few miles away
then on the Bovy clouds hill Lawrence Shaw came to stay
whilst now the guns they fired from lulworth bay
you could hear their roar every day miles away

the streets were busy in the spring
with hawkers all out n marketing
nearby the garrison at Bovington town
where Colonel Carruthers managed the mess
for Queen and crown

whilst Elmes and Samways told the yarns
days long past with blackbirds song
and where as a lad I grew up tall and strong

Ray Wills

The back streets of Poole

Photo courtesy of Poole Museum

The Squires and others lived in the back streets of Poole
with no boots on their feet but had hearts that were true
the lamplighter lady she lit up each morn
so bright and so early to wake you at dawn

the streets there were narrow and the bread they all shared
there were skipping of ropes and singing of bairns
the docks they were rich there and the fishes were sweet
with cockles ans winkles and rags on their feet

the rag and bone man rode the streets every week
with horse cart and shouting to all he did greet
there were neighbour's a plenty to help you in need
with cheerful rich chatter and words oh so sweet

the noblemen passed there and rarely did gain
access to the comforts of their little lanes
there were sailors a courting and maids at your door
kisses and promises and soldiers at war

the streets then were cobbled though none did complain
for the richness was theirs down those narrow lanes
with families large and mothers to gain
with another babe wanting in another broods name

the railways they came there from old Waterloo
with stories of gentlemen said how do you do
but the streets they were poor and the children they too

Ray Wills

Dorset past times

The Amity cinema stood where Woolworth's is today
where Gypsies sold their heather sweet every Saturday
in Poole high street the folks all came some in horse and cart
the folks came early then if they were really smart

on Wareham quay the monkey danced and collected pennies
grand
people would rattle his cage and he would try to bite their hands
the river it froze to block of ice upon a Xmas holiday
kids skated there n frolicked and folks came from miles away

on clouds hill the Arab rider was hidden in his cottage small
there were trees upon the Egdon heath and pines a growing tall
the tanks they rolled there daily and their guns they did roar
close by the Wool brige manor house and its splendid hall

the ducks they waddled in the stream at wool and Durberville
was cool
when hardy wrote of Tess and love and we caught a train to
Poole
rhodendians stretched through Sandfords roads and the postman
came to call
there were histories made in castle corfe then once Romans
roamed the walls

the mad miller of Wareham told his stories there and Lady s,S
Marys rang its bells
whilst Churchill rode to Canford lanes so did the prince of
Wales

Queen Victoria bathed on Weymouth beach and royalty came to call
with Dorset cream and Dorset cake and knobs with crabs at Durdle door

Ray Wills

Dorset steam Fair

Ye old steam fair is here each year
upon the downs with fun and beer
the oil it smells and the tracks are mud
where cars are parked upon the meadows green
the carousels play and delight the scene
the crowds flock here again this year
to buy the goods or storm the gears
there's Gypsy folk and traveller's tales
with smoky air and diesel smells
there's big machines to roll n ride
across the Dorset countryside
where zunners run and play n stare
at all the folks within the fair
with marquee tents and music rock
stalls to sale and gears to lock
amusements rich in fields of green
bikers parades and beauty scenes
crowds of folks flock here each year
to mingle and to enjoy the spirit here
where hills are steep and views are grand
the steam fair spreads across this land

Ray Wills

BEFORE THE HOUSES

From Bourne Valley bottom and along the dirt track
the caravans rumbled to Lodge hills and back
though thick hedges laden full of bramble and gorse
with lovely chestnuts to nibble by our little horse
there at Coy meadows we drank from the stream
little fresh springs and wonders to dream
There were Gypsies at Beales in Bournemouth today
so wel tell you your fortune then be on our way
the village kids saw us and they gave us the eye
in our caravans homes which smoked right up to the sky
With rabbits to ferret and hedgehogs to eat

With songs around the campfire and family to greet
the wheels rolled there daily whilst the stars shone at night
there were folks in their glory with clothes to delight

There was food on the table and rugs on the floor
the candles n lamps lit with designs on the doors
Whilst the music was played with accordion Joe
whilst the songs that we sung were older than dough
There were times which were hard then and folks they did stray
But we were far wiser than many today
the grass grewso course and the daisies were spread
like creation was labelled for the good and the dead

The Queen of the Gypsies was dark and so rare
she had braided long hair and spent nights at Poole fair
the wagons were rich and the lamps they were gold
whilst the little chavs all danced naked upon their tip toes
the chaffinches sung at the break of the day
as we ambled along our stories to say
Now theres just tarmac on Tower Park ridge
where there was once magic with our uncle Sid
For we lived on the heaths then when the land it was free
Before Lord Wimborne sold it to Poole for houses for thee

Ray Wills

Sea View

I took a trip to up on hill
where one could see the view of Poole so still
where pines grew tall and cones were rich
where the banks where steep and the lizards squirmed in and
out the ditch

the school bell rang in woods of green
where children ran and lovers dreamed
high up on top of Constitution hill
where the birds did soar and time stood still

I looked down to old Newtown lands
where the Co op and Wesleyan church it looked so grand
where all Sid Rogers transport lorries stood in line
you could hear the work sirens telling of the times

the old water tower nows in sight
with Phillips quarry's and heaths delights
Once the coal man called and fish man too
from Ringwood road by Alderneys Stainer's shoes

where squirrels did chase and bird did sing
then the cuckoo surprised us every spring
there were orchards rich in sweet delight
where zunners scrumped and the Stanley's did fight

where the bus stop stands next to the loos
at the roundabout top of Sea view *each night*

Ray Wills

The Snakes gone

Their pulling down the snake
taking it apart brick by brick
they're counting all the memories
I heard from billy quick

they've drank there at the Albion
for many years afire
there were Stanley's in the forecourt then
Rogers in the hall

they are selling off the Primitive Methodist
the Wesleyan church on the Ringwood road

their selling off the boozer mate
got to see the monkeys load

the stories that were told there
in Newtown to the kids
there were Gypsies in their caravans
lorries all lined up in Wool lane at uncle Sids

the place will never be the same
the co ops gone long ago
they've sold off their memories to the bankers
come see the sad sad show

the road has lost its vision
where Nobby Watton picked up the fag ends
from out of the gutters
where Knotty sold his caravans
they will never have a Snake again

Ray Wills

WAREHAM

There were cobbled streets in Wareham town
lots of pubs but not a Rose and Crown
there were the Sandpit's and the Saw pits too
plus Carey camp to take kids to

on the quay we swam and fished
where the river Frome swans did glide n kiss
there were walks up winding tracks to Redcliffe n Ridge
across from Stoboroughs farms and the markets sellers bids

the clock it struck upon the hour
there where the old granary did turn the flour
the Mad Miller lived by Warehams walls
where lizards swarmed and yokels talked

nearby in the town where Lawrence stone was laid
theres a tribute to his Moreton grave
the Hardy town where yokel farmers talked
where deer once ran through forests walks

as a child we chased the girls
across those downs and Wareham grassy walls
the Bestwall tracks and Lundigo
the Wareham fair and the Dorchester country show

here kings once rode to Corfe each day
the castle on the hills still there today
on the road to Swanage where Enid Blyton lived
the Purbeck isle and the tales the yokels bid

old Wareham town was mentioned in the Doomsday book
its charms alive still
just take a look

Ray Wills

Westbourne Tales

Where Churchill fell close to the chines
in Westbournes bridge where folks drank wine
with damaged frame and broken ribs
he oft times came to this conker ridge

his friendly aunt lived at Canford lodge
her Guestly name was born in sods
here vagrants walked the fields and rode the land
in caravans and jovial bawdy Gypsy bands

All the viaducts and bridges spanned
with red brick walls built by Irish navvy hands
where labourer craftsmen and Newtown lads
blessed the soil and kissed the flesh neath bonnie rags

where noble lords and common crew
rode to the docks at olde town Poole
where squires did feast upon their gain
whilst poor barefoot children ran the lanes

Ray Wills

Enid Blytons Days

I recall the secret seven and the famous five
those Enid Blyton stories kept our childhood so alive
With their tales of pirate caves and hidden treasure troves
maps with crosses on and walks upon Lulworth cove
the Sandy shores and walks of Sandbanks downs
the Studland beach with the dunes so white
the rocky cliffs and walls of the Dorset towns
the steep n hilly walks of the Purbeck mounds
the secret tunnels we all took
the rambling countryside around
the bikes our dogs the kings and crowns
the Englishness of the Swanage beach
with the view of Wessex just out of reach
the grassy meadows where we all played
the Punch and Judy shows
on our summer holidays.

Ray Wills

DORSET BREED

Dorset blue vinney with doorsteps to spread
crusty ole knobs and words quick to shed
country lanes twisting and rambling free
green open country with scenes by the sea
Thatched barns and cottages with chapels of rest
old country squires with stables so blessed
paddocks harvests and brooks running free
countryside meadows lead to the sea
church bells that ring out each Sunday morn
market stalls plenty and crops full of corn
all pretty maidens waiting to dance

kisses on lips and young mens last chance
willows and oaks with birch growing free
commons and woodlands with rivers by sea
fishes to catch and coves to explore
castles on hillsides and Hardy and more
old country yokels and yarn for to spin
gypsy tale memories and riddle dee whims
across country rambles and blackberry thorns
dock leaves and stingers and old faded porn
Crafted and weavers and dances on grass
bee stings and honey to bless you perchance
dogs in the farmyard and hens in the coop
farmers in bed and fox on the loose
Old crafts and new deals and artists and friends
poets and writers and old fashioned men
twisting and turning the roads and the bends
Turners great pictures and poets uill pens
Fashioned and crafted and set free to share
the writers and artists the fun of the fairs
the stickle back fishes and the newts in a jar
old uns to listen to and old tales to tell.

Ray Wills

BLUEBIRD CARAVANS

I painted caravans for Mr Knott
I sprayed horse boxes quite a lot
from magnets to grand Pacific hues
Swiss cottages and Caravanettes too
they went abroad to States from Poole
I decorated the kitchen and the chassis I did spray
they told me that in peace work I earned the highest pay

There were Gypsy wagons on the heath
a barber shops in Newtown and that's where I cut my teeth
I was the highest paid boy in the factory
I sprayed another horsebox then I ran home for tea

Mr Knott he had yachts and he sailed them in Poole bay
then he cut our our wages by twenty per cent reduced our pay
when we all went on strike it was on the tv
I was famous at last interviewed by the BBC

I met all the big boys from the unions and press
in my CND stance and my American hair and denim dress
I stood on the picket line and I answered the call
but the battle was lost when mr Knott sacked one and all

Ray Wills

ONE OF THE LADS

Cockleshell heroes on sandcastle bays
walks in the sunlight and children at play
grass in the meadows and cows in the corn
church steeples views and the country's remains

Secluded places in forestry walks
farmers and yokels all durzet talk
tractors and trailers boys on the spree
gals in the haystack talking with me

Cider with Rosie and kisses with Jane
warm breasts to hold down country lanes

cow pats and tall grass and places to see
out in the country with Susie and me

Pubs with thatched roofs and pints left to pull
tables of oak and beams running through
gardens of roses and music so sweet
oh to be young with gals at your feet

Castles on hilltops with true Purbeck views
walks in the country from Wareham to Poole
air it is salty and wind it is free
rides on the ferry with Sandra and me

Boys playing cricket against the church wall
Girls playing hockey green knickers tucked and all
lads playing hookey and girls telling tales
oh the weather was climate and the inks in the wells

The Schoolmasters cane and teachers best pet
out on the farm for eggs left to get
cockerels a crowing and the hens they did lay
days out in the barn with Heather and Ray

Ray Wills

THE BATMAN

Once I was a batman
at the officers request
I ironed all their uniforms
so they looked their very best

I polished up their brasses
made their beds and cleaned their rooms
I lit up all the fires
put on their favourite tunes
I brought them tea in bed
then nursed them when their drunk
I organized their day
though I was just a punk

I polished all their shoes
brought their papers too
but I was just so innocent then
before I read the news

I worked inside the Officers mess
at their request in the officers best home
I was young n naive then
just one kid on his own

Then later I got educated
I saw the miners strikes
I saw the poverty in Biafra
thats things I did not like

I read upon George Orwell
heard Lennon and Zimmerman
they taught me peace and demonstrated
just how to understand that war was just a consequence
of some big brother plan
then I left home to wander
learned to be a man

Ray Wills

School Days

Bill Rogers courtesy of Lynda Stuchberry

There was a little tuck shop
around the corner from Branksome heath school
with liquorice reels of skipping ropes
and gaudy sweet false teeth too

I went to school at Branksome heath
when I was a small wee lad
I drew pictures of naked ladies then
oh I was so very bad

We waved the flags on Empire day
played marbles on the ground
picture post cards we called flicks
we listened to the band

We often walked to school
or rode the bus number eight
we had those rucksacks on our backs
parents waved us from our gates

We said our prayers there daily
sang the schools own song
we all had recreation
and we all just got along

Our teachers all were so called wise men
we recited maths tables and weather then
knew our place and more
we always did as we were told
or wed all get what for

Ray Wills

GYPSY LAD

She married a Gypsy with big roving eyes
he gave her his heather and told her his lies
he was born on the common one hour afore morn
he told her he loved her then left her at dawn

He worked in the fairgrounds and ponies he rode
he was a one for the ladies and the gal down the road
he drove a big cart and he told you a yarn
he was noble and famous but his breeches were worn

He wore those big earrings and talked diddy coy
he loved all the ladies and gave em the eye
he mixed with the Coopers,the Mabeys and Kings
though his name was George Castle he was the head of the ring
he could sale you a story and tell you a lie
say it was the real Truth with that look in the eye

His family made flowers and kettles and tins
he was raised on old Canford just where the old warblers sings
he lived in a caravan with its high wooden roof
he walked with a limp and his language was uncouth
he swore and he told some terrible lies
though the gals loved his blarney and his lovely dark eyes

They hung all their washing on the bramble bush free
they had a dozen juk dogs and lots of new forest ponies
his mother was called Queenie and his father a king
they said he had him a fortune inside his gold ring

his pals came from Surrey and sold at the Downs for that's what
he said
as he told her her fortune then took her to bed

The bed it was bouncy and the springs they did squeak
he loved her there twice nightly each day of the week
she was a dreamer pretty and cool
some say a diamond and some say a fool
but he was only a Gypsy who grew up in Newtown near Poole

Ray Wills

KID IN WAREHAM

When I was a kid in Wareham
I played upon the high grass walls
the grass was green and high then
you had one hell of a long ways to fall

We caught lizards there daily
caught minnows on the quay
I rang the church bells on Sundays
we had rabbit pie for our tea

The cuckoos lived in Stoborough
then when they let them out the meadows gate
on Thursday Easter fun day
we ate hot Cross buns
on the burrow there at Creche
and we all stayed up till late

We collected chestnuts down Home lane
played conkers whilst at school
the Head masters name was Stuckey
old Samways played the fool

The kids all loved the river
then we had the fair
I dated lots of pretty gals
with ringlets in their hair

David Mellor I once baby sat
he became a con MP

then David Best turned down Man United
guess he thought that he knew best
dont know what he was

Thomas Hardy wrote about the town
the place I love the best
when I was a kid in Wareham
they put me through the test

Ray Wills

Kinsons History

The old school once stood upon the site of the present village
green
Whilst cricket wickets fell nearby on the local scene
Two master batsmen went to war in France
Reverend Sharpe oversaw it all perchance

Village lads Jesse Short and William Hicks
said to have done the work of six
when they pulled Kaiser Bill out of the Meads ditch
he had just returned from visiting Lady Wimborne Churchills
aunt
oh how that story got about

At Canfords fine estates its home of deer and chance

Gulliver had property at West Moors and near Brook lane
he was such a well respected gentleman and a smuggler
throughout Poole
He had pubs at Longham and at Kinson Howes
the kids collected chestnuts from Pelhams fall
where stream it ran by the Pelhams house Millhams lanes high
wall
A Tulip tree was gifted from Newfound folks many miles away
It travelled here from Michigan to Pelhams lovely grounds
where a Gentle mans handshake was agreed n swore
Pelham was chosen to be for use by common folks n all
Kinson was to remain in Poole until 1932
All part of a great heath land in the domain of Poole
where chestnuts grew amongst twisting lanes
home of chirps and moos

Ray Wills

Farmers Boy

Yesterday I took a walk down winding tracks
Where birdsong greets the mornings realms
Where reeds and heathers do bestow
A pleasure garden all on show

I gazed on hills spread so green
Where lambs and seagulls paint the scene
Where clouds of cotton wool do show
The joys of life all spread below

Across the heaths of rabbits runs
Where fox gave chase whilst farmers sons
Sang all their songs like folks in prayer
and wallowed in the beauty there

I spied the tractor oer the soil
The fields of grain across the moors
The lilac trees and nettles sweet
Where tramps and ladies trod their feet

The seas of spray where fish do dance
To sands of time and pebbles chance
To sailboats riding on the spray
Where the sunshine bright across the bay

The church tower clock doth chime the hour
Their bells do ring across the stour
Whilst zunners run from school this day
Whilst lovers frolic in the hay

I spy the village pond and old water pump
the five barred gate where walkers humped their rucksacks
and stout poles of fine regard
Just a stone throw away from farmers yard

Where the gander geese gave chase to Mary Jane
Whilst the dogs did bark and lords did monies gain
Where stoned wall walks were set in sand
Where Hardy wrote and Barnes statue still doth stand

Where the market hawkers gave full guest
Whilst us zunners ran amongst the bests
Where today s pubs and cafes do imitate
Those histories of landed gentries fates

The walks I took that summers day
Across the Purbeck right of way
Where travellers rest and shoulders of muttons rich
In its histories lessons spread across the ditch

While warblers sang and fat lizards squirmed
The adders and the shiny slow worms
The master poet was lost in joy
When I was but a child and farmers boy.

Ray Wills

THE GYPSY STORY TELLER

Ray Wills

The Gypsy story teller he could tell a yarn
chickens in the alleyways
and cattle in the barn
there were vardos on the hillsides
and benders on the downs
groups of chavvies running free
and the Queen she wore a crown
the heaths were wild and full of broom
with yellow scented furze
there were rabbits in the mead there

and foxes for to curse
the pegs were made of wood then
and the heather for your luck
there accordion's were playing
and the horses they did buck
the hills were full of beauty
and the downs were rambling runs
there were chapels full of local folk
and ladies hair in buns
the yokel talked in durzet tones
and told a yarn to all
the Gypsy story teller lived upon the moors
the Gypsy story teller
could tell a yarn or two
about Gypsy kings and queens
and local yeomen too
the Hurdy Gurdy played a tune
in towns then far and wide
with barefoot chavvies running free
and broomstick Gypsy brides
The Kings and Castle families
with Jeff's and Whites in tow
old Sankey Ward built houses
and Trent's sold cars and loads
the Gypsy story teller told tales of long ago
when Gypsies roamed this land
and toffs their wealth did grow
the Gypsy story teller told yarns
to children small
old folks and families alike

awaken to the call
the vardos decked in artistry
and wooden steps to sit
whilst pots and pens were full of grub
for little mush

Ray Wills

Cavalier Days

Photo courtesy of Terry Andrews

I still can recall those beat-ifull days
the dances at the Naffi and the ship where they played
the beat it was loud and the music was cool
we were all the wiser that side of Poole

the songs that we sung and the music went twang
our heartbeats were quick and it went with a bang
the long hair and drainpipes with Beatle new boots
we were young but much wiser n not old in the tooth

the Durberville hall and the cricket pitch green
the sounds of the guns from the Bovington scenes
the laughter and frolics and ballroom attires
the mods and the rockers along with the squires

the music was rich then as they strummed a few chords
from trips to the oceans on queen Elizabeth's world
the band played a medley of Beatles and rock
where teenagers gathered in their best gear and smocks

near lulworths great bay and Durdles wide door
where tanks they did roll and emblems cross swords
the garrison nearby with its history of Shaw
close by the river banks where hardy explored

they drunk from the ship inn and danced on the floor
in the old hut that's not there any more
the guys they had long hair and the girls beehive too
they snogged on the dance floor close to the loos

the music they played was out of this world
they sang all the standards and we heard every word
the Morley's and Jones boy sung out the songs
wel never forget them as we sang them along

the nights then were free and full of good cheer
as we ate up our crisps and drunk of fine beer
those days are gone now but the music lives on
in the minds of the dreamers who still sing the songs

the cavalier days and the barbecue sets
the walks in the country
we will never forget

Ray Wills

CYRIL WOOD COURT

Photo courtesy of East Borough Housing

On Cyril Wood Court the music did play
you could hear the guitars twang by night and by day
where poets and writers n potters and artists did paint
on the streets of Bere Regis oh twas so very quaint
and here folks did often frequent
Some boozers did pub crawl n some folks they did hide
some wrote their stories racy and wild
others walked n they talked through the rich countryside
they crafted their pots and their music was rich
from bohemian rhapsodies to the works of little mix
some folks were classical pianos did play
the works of the masters whilst others did say
that the artists were hidden in their rooms far away
Some were masters of classics and some they were wild
some sang at the local and the village open mike days
others wrote fancy verse and some were so wild for days

The rock n roll guitars twanged in the night in Hendrix style
haze and creative craze
On Cyril Wood Court it was quiet these days
since the lock down began
yet the music still played

Ray Wills

ABOUT THE AUTHOR

Ray Wills was born in Newtown Poole Dorset in 1945. Ray childhood and early youth was spent in Dorset on the Mannings heath Poole and at Wareham. After leaving school at Kemp Welch Parkstone Poole. His first job was as a painter and chassis sprayer for Bluebird Caravans the largest caravan industry in the world.

Numerous other jobs followed including time as an Officers Batman in Bovington Dorset before joining Community Service Volunteers and entering the field of child play provision. For many decades Ray worked closely with the National Playing Fields Association establishing very many childrens adventure playgrounds throughout the UK in inner cities and rural communities. Gaining qualifications including Royal Society of Arts Diploma in Management and City and Guilds. Ray was a founder member of Poole Poetry group. His publications have included writing contributions to and editing "The Gypsy Storyteller" anthology for Francis Boutle Publisher, "Romance in the Everglades" poetry anthology- publisher by xpress publications. Ray is an authority on the history of the Gypsy community as a member of Kushti Bok. Ray has self published with Lulu..com and these have included "The Canford Chronicles "a poetry Anthology, "Where the River Bends", "Ventures in Childs Play" and "The Gypsy Camp". He also frequently writes articles for magazines including "Traveller Times" and "Play and Playground". He at present lives within a community of artists, writers and musicians in the village of Bere Regis Wareham in Dorset and he continues to give regular talks on local history and poetry readings throughout Dorset .

Printed in Poland
by Amazon Fulfillment
Poland Sp. z o.o., Wrocław

61777565R00098